Make Way for Animals!

A World of Wildlife Crossings

Meeg Pincus

illustrated by Bao Luu

Millbrook Press / Minneapolis

Mom, this one's for you. Thanks for always being my bridge over troubled waters.
—M.P.

To everyone who reads this book, thank you for being the motivation and helping
me to realize my dream of working as an illustrator.
—B.L.

Millbrook Press™
An imprint of Lerner Publishing Group, Inc.
241 First Avenue North
Minneapolis, MN 55401 USA

For reading levels and more information, look up this title at www.lernerbooks.com.

Back matter photos by: juerginho/Shutterstock.com, p. 30T; Paul Juser/Shutterstock.com, p. 30B;
Justine Emm/Shutterstock.com, p. 31T; kavram/Shutterstock.com, p. 31B.

Designed by Viet Chu.
Main body text set in VAG Rounded Std. Typeface provided by Adobe Systems.
The illustrations in this book were created digitally using Adobe Photoshop on a Wacom Cintiq.

Library of Congress Cataloging-in-Publication Data

Names: Pincus, Meeg, author. | Luu, Bao, 1995– illustrator.
Title: Make way for animals! : a world of wildlife crossings / Meeg Pincus ; illustrated by Bao Luu.
Description: Minneapolis : Millbrook Press, [2022] | Includes bibliographical references. |
    Audience: Ages 5–9 | Audience: Grades 2–3 | Summary: "Around the world, roads have cut off
    animals from the resources they need to survive. Fortunately, this problem has also inspired
    some creative solutions! Take a tour of wildlife crossings from badger bridges to penguin
    pipelines." —Provided by publisher.
Identifiers: LCCN 2021024696 (print) | LCCN 2021024697 (ebook) | ISBN 9781541589384 (lib. bdg.) |
    ISBN 9781728445359 (ebook)
Subjects: LCSH: Wildlife crossings—Juvenile literature. | Animals—Effect of roads on—Juvenile
    literature.
Classification: LCC SK356.W54 P566 2022 (print) | LCC SK356.W54 (ebook) | DDC 333.95/4—dc23

LC record available at https://lccn.loc.gov/2021024696
LC ebook record available at https://lccn.loc.gov/2021024697

Manufactured in the United States of America
1-47472-48028-8/3/2021

The road is a visitor.

—Philosophy of the Peoples Way wildlife crossings team,
Flathead Indian Reservation, Montana, United States

Hilversum, Netherlands

European badgers. Forest foragers. Mischievous pack mammals.

They'd wandered these woodlands since the days of woolly mammoths, seeking food and shelter.

Then the roads came, blocking their way.

How could the badgers find meals and homes now?

Oamaru, New Zealand

Little blue fairy penguins. Dynamic divers. Puniest penguins on the planet.

They'd swum this small stretch of sea for thousands of years, gliding ashore to burrow, nest, and molt.

Then the roads came, blocking their way.

How could the penguins make their nests now?

Christmas Island, Indian Ocean

Red crabs. Claw clickers. Millions migrating together.

They'd trekked from forest to coast for generations to release their eggs in the sea.

Then the roads came, blocking their way.

How could the crabs get their eggs to the ocean now?

Nanyuki, Kenya

African elephants. Continent crossers. World's largest land animals.

They'd rumbled through here since ancient times searching for mates and fresh water sources.

Then the roads came, blocking their way.

How could the elephants find mates and drinking water now?

Around the world, city highways and country roads have cut through natural spaces.

Cars and trucks have caused tragic crashes (and lots of roadkill).

Wild animals have lost safe access to what they need to survive.

In some of these places, people have asked,

How can we help wild animals when our roads block their way?

And they've come up with solutions . . .

In the Netherlands, bridges for the badgers . . .

The Netherlands' six hundred animal bridges saved the European badgers from extinction—and help bison, elk, wild boar, and other critters as well!

In New Zealand, a pipeline for the penguins . . .

Little blue fairy penguins coast ashore in groups called rafts, from a few to a hundred at a time, then cross through this pipeline to get to their nests.

On Christmas Island, crossings for the crabs . . .

Each year when the moon signals migration time, forty million crabs follow a human-made maze and thirty-six crossings that lead them safely to the sea.

In Kenya, an underpass for the elephants!

This underpass reconnects wild land for seven thousand elephants whose natural instinct is to travel 30 miles (48 km) a day.

These solutions have a name: wildlife crossings.

On six of the seven continents and in forty-three of the fifty US states,
wildlife crossings provide safe routes around roads for all kinds of creatures.

Some wildlife crossings help animals cross beneath the roads . . .

A detour for deer in Canada.

The forty-four wildlife crossings in Banff, Canada, have greatly reduced car crashes with deer, moose, and caribou, saving many animal and human lives.

A secret tunnel for spotted salamanders in Massachusetts.

Ten US states have special programs to create tunnels like this for amphibians—including salamanders, newts, frogs, and toads—so they can safely bypass roads.

Some wildlife crossings help animals cross above the roads . . .

A rope bridge for ringtail possums in Australia.

Mother possums with baby joeys in their pouches
use this rope bridge to stay away from roads.
Then later, they teach their joeys to use it as well.

A natural canopy for night monkeys in Peru.

Kinkajous, squirrels, and dwarf porcupines
also cross this tree bridge to avoid oil pipelines
that divide their rain forest habitat.

Some wildlife crossings even help animals cross barriers in the water . . .

A ladder for leaping fish in Japan.

This fish ladder was built thirty years ago to help endangered Ryukyu ayu-fish scale a human-made dam and continue their natural path upstream.

And some wildlife crossings help animals cross through the sky!

A passageway for pollinators in Norway.

This world's first "bee highway" provides rooftop structures with food and shelter to keep bees flying safely above the city.

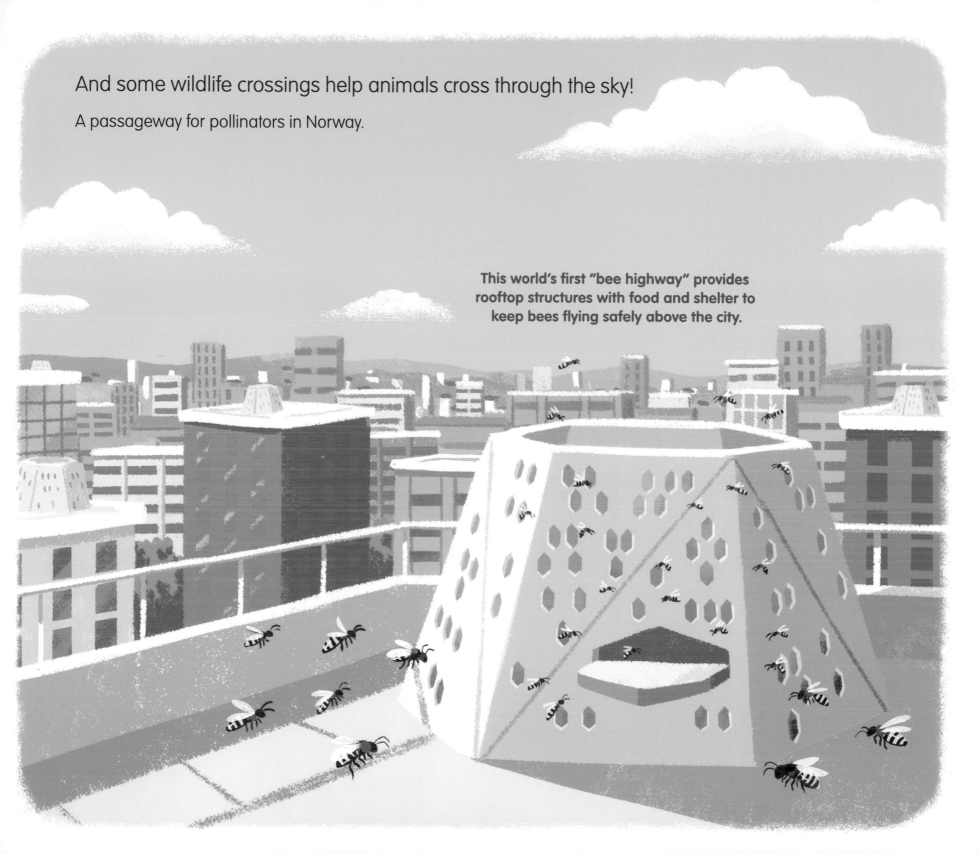

It takes all kinds of people to bring animal overpasses and underpasses to life.

Activists and architects, fundraisers and field researchers.
Civil engineers and scientists. Local leaders and construction crews.

They dream up these passageways and do
the work to make them happen.

Thanks to wildlife crossings . . .

Badgers can find food.

Penguins can make nests.

Crabs can release eggs.

Elephants can meet mates.

Creatures large and small, across the globe, can survive.

When planning new roads, people must say: *make way for animals!*

And then, we must create the way.

The wonderful world of wildlife crossings

A *wildlife crossing* is a human-made structure, usually spanning over or under a road. There are also *wildlife corridors*, which can combine protected natural lands and human-made structures.

Both crossings and corridors allow wild animals to migrate and move freely, safe from traffic. Protecting natural migration patterns and animal behaviors keeps species alive and ecosystems in balance, which helps humans, plants, and animals.

European cities built the first wildlife crossings in the 1950s. Today, in the United States, there are two million car accidents involving wild animals yearly, causing many thousands of animal and human injuries and deaths. More cities in the US and around the world are designing and building wildlife crossings to combat this problem.

Wildlife crossings, like this one in Germany, are becoming part of the planning when some new highways are built.

The Nutty Narrows Bridge has been keeping squirrels safe from vehicles in Washington State for about sixty years!

Sometimes one person sparks the creation of a wildlife crossing:

- In Washington State, a contractor named Amos Peters designed and built a crossing for squirrels called the Nutty Narrows Bridge above his small town's main street in 1963. (Squirrels still use it today!)

- In Japan, an engineer named Koichi Otake was so inspired after working on a suspension bridge to help tiny dormice cross safely over a road that he started a whole organization to promote wildlife crossings around his country.

- In Los Angeles, California, Beth Pratt, California regional executive director for the National Wildlife Federation, heard that wildlife biologists had been asking for years for an animal bridge over L.A.'s 101 Freeway to save the area's endangered mountain lions from extinction. So she set off on a mission to make it happen. She launched a successful campaign, #SaveLACougars, to raise millions of dollars for what's slated to be the world's largest wildlife crossing, expected to be completed by 2024.

When many people come together, entire networks of wildlife crossings can protect animals along major highways or throughout regions. This has happened in several places, including these three:

A community can come together to support animal crossings, as was the case for the Peoples Way wildlife crossing network in Montana.

Some protected wildlife areas, such as Canada's Banff National Park, have overpasses and underpasses to shield animals from vehicles.

- Montana, USA. When the government wanted to expand a highway through the wilderness of the Flathead Indian Reservation, leaders from the Confederated Salish and Kootenai Tribes spent ten years pushing back and talking with national and state officials. Finally, they all worked together—using the philosophy of "the road as a visitor" and "Spirit of Place"—to let the land shape the road's design. They also created the Peoples Way wildlife crossing network, which includes forty-three animal crossings under and over the new highway, plus nearly 30 miles [48 km] of fencing, to protect animals, plants, and waterways.

- The Netherlands. Government officials, wildlife scientists, businesspeople, and architects collaborated to find ways to protect the endangered European badgers. Now this country's six hundred wildlife crossings—the most of any country!—protect badgers and all kinds of other animals, including bison and wild boar.

- Banff, Canada. When roads were slated to run through the vast mountains and meadows of Canada's Banff National Park, a whole team designed and built forty-four wildlife crossings to protect grizzly bears, deer, moose, cougars, coyotes, lynx, wolves, and wolverines.

Wildlife crossings are a beautiful example of how people and animals can live in harmony. Are there any where you live? If you're not sure, do some digging and find out!

Design Your Own Wildlife Crossing

For a fun project, you can design your own wildlife crossing for any kind of wild animal in any place you can think of! It could be a bridge, a tunnel, a natural canopy, or something else.

Draw it, sculpt it from clay, build it with Legos—use your creativity! If it's for your own community, consider sharing your idea with elected officials or city planners.

Selected Bibliography

Agence France-Presse. "Oslo Creates World's First 'Highway' to Protect Endangered Bees." *Guardian* (US edition), June 25, 2015. https://www.theguardian.com/environment/2015/jun/25/oslo-creates-worlds-first-highway-to-protect-endangered-bees.

Beckmann, Jon, Anthony Clevenger, Marcel Huijser, and Jodi Hilty, eds. *Safe Passages: Highways, Wildlife and Habitat Connectivity.* Washington, DC: Island, 2010.

Cullinane, Susannah. "NZ Builds Underpass for Little Penguins to Safely Cross Road." CNN, November 12, 2016. https://www.cnn.com/2016/11/12/asia/nz-penguin-underpass/index.html.

"Other Crossing Brigades." Harris Center for Conservation Education. Updated April 16, 2021. https://harriscenter.org/programs-and-education/citizen-science/salamander-crossing-brigades/other-crossing-brigade-programs.

Pratt, Beth, California regional executive director for the National Wildlife Federation and lead of #SaveLACougars wildlife crossing campaign. Telephone interview, January 11, 2018.

Salisbury, Claire. "In Peru, Canopy Bridges Keep Rainforest Animals Connected over Gas Pipeline." Scroll.in, August 5, 2017. https://scroll.in/article/846008/in-peru-canopy-bridges-keep-rainforest-animals-connected-over-a-gas-pipeline.

Steyn, Paul. "Urban Wildlife Corridors Could Save Africa's Free-Roaming Elephants." *National Geographic Society Newsroom* (blog), December 12, 2013. https://blog.nationalgeographic.org/2013/12/12/urban-wildlife-corridors-could-save-africas-free-roaming-elephants/.

Wells, Ken. "Wildlife Crossings Get a Whole New Look." *Wall Street Journal,* June 20, 2017.

"Wildlife Crossings." National Geographic Resource Library, July 16, 2019. https://www.nationalgeographic.org/article/wildlife-crossings/.

"Wildlife-Vehicle Collision Reduction Study: Report to Congress." US Department of Transportation, Federal Highway Administration, August 2008. https://www.fhwa.dot.gov/publications/research/safety/08034/.

"A Wild Way to Move—Banff National Park." YouTube video, 3:52. Posted by Parks Canada on June 13, 2014. https://www.youtube.com/watch?v=9JX6cqME6Hw.